Oklahoma Sooners IQ: The Ultimate Test of True Fandom

Scott Cooper
& Keith Gaddie

2011 Edition
(Volume I)

This title is part of the IQ sports trivia book series, which is a trademark of Black Mesa Publishing, LLC.

Cataloging-in-Publication Data is available from the Library of Congress.

ISBN: 978-0-9837922-1-5
First edition, first printing.

Cover photo and design by BMP.

Black Mesa Publishing, LLC
Florida
David Horne and Marc CB Maxwell
Black.Mesa.Publishing@gmail.com

www.blackmesabooks.com

Introduction

If there is a temple of college football, it might be found in Norman, Oklahoma. For more than 100 years, the central Oklahoma town has been home to one of the elite programs of college football. There are few teams (if any) that can claim the flag of NCAA football supremacy like the Sooners.

The home place for Heisman Trophy winning players, record-breaking coaches, and super fanatic fans, the University of Oklahoma is as proud of its football program as its heritage. The Sooners have laid claim to several national records, which not only are a true testament to its players, but to a program that grooms football greatness.

This book will remind readers and fans what it took to make OU football a winning tradition. It will also bring back memories of players and coaches who for several years or one bright shinny Saturday etched their name in Sooner football lore.

Enjoy this trip down OU Sooner football memory lane.

Boomer Sooner!

Oklahoma Sooners Trivia IQ

QUESTION 1: Which OU head coach was *NOT* an OU assistant before becoming head coach?
 a) Barry Switzer
 b) Bud Wilkinson
 c) Gary Gibbs
 d) Bob Stoops

QUESTION 2: Which OU player did *NOT* win the Heisman Trophy?
 a) Jason White
 b) Joe Washington
 c) Billy Sims
 d) Steve Owens

QUESTION 3: What year did OU start playing football?
 a) 1907
 b) 1900
 c) 1890
 d) 1895

QUESTION 4: When was OU's last undefeated season?
 a) 2000
 b) 1974
 c) 2005
 d) 1985

QUESTION 5: What years did OU pull off its NCAA record-setting 47 game win streak?
 a) 1950-1954
 b) 1971-1974
 c) 1953-1957
 d) 2000-2004

"In pro football you're a number. If you don't play well, you're gone and no one cares. But in college, coaches recruit young men and ask them to become part of their family and help you become a productive citizen for the next 30, 40, 50 years of your life. Your coaches help you develop into something you can be proud of and they are there for life."
— *Barry Switzer*

QUESTION 6: What year was OU's first televised game?
- a) 1950
- b) 1952
- c) 1960
- d) 1957

QUESTION 7: Which Bowl game has OU played in the most?
- a) Sugar
- b) Fiesta
- c) Cotton
- d) Orange

QUESTION 8: Which OU player did *NOT* win the Outland Trophy?
- a) Rick Bryan
- b) Lee Roy Selmon
- c) Jamal Brown
- d) J.D. Roberts

QUESTION 9: Which OU player was *NOT* taken as the number one overall pick in the NFL draft?
  a) Billy Sims
  b) Steve Owens
  c) Lee Roy Selmon
  d) Sam Bradford

QUESTION 10: Which OU linebacker won the first two Butkus awards?
  a) Teddy Lehman
  b) Rocky Calmus
  c) George Cumby
  d) Brian Bosworth

QUESTION 11: Only once has OU had players win the Heisman and Outland trophies in the same year. Who were they?
  a) Billy Sims and Greg Roberts
  b) Jamal Brown and Jason White
  c) Billy Vessels and J.D. Roberts
  d) Sam Bradford and Trent Williams

QUESTION 12: Which OU player is in the NFL Hall of Fame?
  a) Tommy McDonald
  b) Billy Sims
  c) Keith Jackson
  d) Steve Owens

QUESTION 13: Which OU coach also coached the Saint Louis Cardinals in the NFL?
  a) Barry Switzer
  b) Chuck Fairbanks
  c) Bud Wilkinson
  d) Bennie Owen

QUESTION 14: Which coach has the most OU victories?
  a) Bob Stoops
  b) Barry Switzer

c) Bennie Owen
d) Bud Wilkinson

QUESTION 15: Who coached OU the longest?
a) Bob Stoops
b) Barry Switzer
c) Bennie Owen
d) Bud Wilkinson

QUESTION 16: Which team did OU beat in the Orange Bowl for the 1985 national championship?
a) Florida State
b) Michigan
c) Notre Dame
d) Penn State

QUESTION 17: Which school joined OU in suing the NCAA over television rights in 1982?
a) Georgia
b) Notre Dame
c) Texas
d) Nebraska

QUESTION 18: What year did Oklahoma Memorial Stadium open?
a) 1970
b) 1955
c) 1929
d) 1923

QUESTION 19: Which player set NCAA records for most yards rushing and most carriers as a freshman?
a) Marcus Dupree
b) Billy Sims
c) Adrian Peterson
d) Stanley Wilson

QUESTION 20: Which player set the NCAA record for punt return yards in a game?
- a) Ryan Broyles
- b) Antonio Perkins
- c) Darrell Ray
- d) Joe Washington

QUESTION 21: Which OU kicker holds the school record for most extra points in a season?
- a) Uwe Von Shaman
- b) Tim Lashar
- c) Jimmy Stevens
- d) Scott Blanton

QUESTION 22: Which OU head coach has not won 100 games?
- a) Bob Stoops
- b) Chuck Fairbanks
- c) Bennie Owen
- d) Bud Wilkinson

QUESTION 23: Which head coach died after his first year at OU?
- a) Gomer Jones
- b) Jim Tatum
- c) Howard Schnellenberger
- d) Jim Mackenzie

QUESTION 24: Which Heisman Trophy winner was also an Academic All-American?
- a) Sam Bradford
- b) Jason White
- c) Billy Sims
- d) Steve Owens

QUESTION 25: Who did OU beat in the Orange Bowl to win the 2000 national championship?
- a) Michigan
- b) Ohio State

c) Florida State
d) Alabama

"If you are going to be a champion, you must be willing to pay a greater price than your opponent."
— *Bud Wilkinson*

QUESTION 26: Who did OU beat in the Orange Bowl to win the 1975 national championship?
a) Florida State
b) Michigan
c) Texas
d) Notre Dame

QUESTION 27: Due to a scheduling change, which conference foe did OU have to play two years in a row on the road in 1986 and 1987?
a) Nebraska
b) Texas
c) Oklahoma State
d) Missouri

QUESTION 28: Which year did OU have four players drafted in the NFL's first round?
a) 2010
b) 1988
c) 1970
d) 1955

QUESTION 29: In 1979, Billy Sims missed winning his second Heisman Trophy to which player?
- a) Earl Campbell
- b) Charles White
- c) Hershel Walker
- d) Marcus Allen

QUESTION 30: Which coach replaced Barry Switzer in 1989?
- a) Howard Schnellenberger
- b) John Blake
- c) Bob Stoops
- d) Gary Gibbs

QUESTION 31: OU played this team twice during the 1978 season and bowl game.
- a) Texas
- b) Oklahoma State
- c) Nebraska
- d) Stanford

QUESTION 32: Who is the oldest Selmon brother?
- a) Dewey
- b) Lee Roy
- c) Lucious
- d) None, they were born on the same day

QUESTION 33: What is the record for most points scored by OU in one game?
- a) 179
- b) 111
- c) 90
- d) 82

QUESTION 34: Who was the first OU player to win the Jim Thorpe award for the nation's best defensive back?
- a) Ricky Dixon
- b) Roy Williams

c) Darrell Ray
d) Derrick Strait

QUESTION 35: What is the record for most punts by OU in one game?
a) 10
b) 13
c) 18
d) 20

QUESTION 36: Which NFL quarterback did Jason White beat out for the 2003 Heisman Trophy?
a) Eli Manning
b) Ben Roethlisberger
c) Matt Leinart
d) Byron Leftwich

QUESTION 37: Which OU player later served in the Oklahoma Legislature?
a) Jack Mildren
b) J.C. Watts
c) Dewey Selmon
d) Todd Thomsen

QUESTION 38: Which OU player holds the record for career starts at quarterback?
a) Jack Mildren
b) Sam Bradford
c) Cale Gundy
d) Jamelle Holieway

QUESTION 39: Against which team did Barry Switzer earn his first head coaching win?
a) Baylor
b) Texas
c) Arizona
d) Missouri

QUESTION 40: In which Texas town did Billy Sims play high school football?
- a) Houston
- b) Denton
- c) Tyler
- d) Hooks

QUESTION 41: Where did OU head coach Bud Wilkinson play college football?
- a) Oklahoma
- b) Minnesota
- c) Texas
- d) Stanford

QUESTION 42: Who did OU play in its first trip to a bowl game, the Orange Bowl in 1938?
- a) Florida State
- b) Penn State
- c) Tennessee
- d) Pittsburgh

QUESTION 43: Who was the only team to beat OU in its 1950 national championship season?
- a) Texas
- b) Nebraska
- c) Alabama
- d) Kentucky

QUESTION 44: Who was the only team to beat OU in its 1985 national championship season?
- a) Miami
- b) Nebraska
- c) USC
- d) UCLA

QUESTION 45: Who was the only team to beat OU in its 1975 national championship season?
   a) Kansas
   b) Missouri
   c) Texas
   d) Nebraska

QUESTION 46: Which kicker holds the OU record for the longest made field goal in school history?
   a) Uwe von Schamann
   b) Tim Lashar
   c) R.D. Lashar
   d) Tony DiRienzo

QUESTION 47: What was the final score in the 1971 OU vs. Nebraska game labeled the Game of the Century?
   a) Nebraska 35 OU 31
   b) OU 35 Nebraska 31
   c) Nebraska 28 OU 24
   d) OU 28 Nebraska 21

QUESTION 48: What year was the Sooner Schooner introduced at games?
   a) 1947
   b) 1964
   c) 1975
   d) 1980

QUESTION 49: Who beat OU in the 2004 Sugar Bowl for the national championship?
   a) USC
   b) LSU
   c) BYU
   d) UCLA

QUESTION 50: Who drafted Lee Roy Selmon for the first pick in the 1976 draft?
a) Dallas Cowboys
b) Pittsburgh Steelers
c) Tampa Bay
d) Oakland Raiders

"If a team is to reach its potential, each player must be willing to subordinate his personal goals to the good of the team."
— Bud Wilkinson

QUESTION 51: Which NFL team drafted Billy Sims for the first pick in the 1980 draft?
a) Miami Dolphins
b) Seattle Seahawks
c) Washington Redskins
d) Detroit Lions

QUESTION 52: In 1980, OU set a modern-day school record for most points scored in a game, 82. Who was the opponent?
a) Colorado
b) Texas
c) Nebraska
d) Kansas

QUESTION 53: OU player Bob Kalsu was the only active player killed in the Vietnam War. What NFL team drafted him in 1968?
a) Dallas Cowboys
b) Buffalo Bills

c) San Diego Chargers
d) Baltimore Colts

QUESTION 54: Which Texas head coach played at OU?
  a) Fred Akers
  b) Mack Brown
  c) David McWilliams
  d) Darrell Royal

QUESTION 55: Who did OU beat for its first Rose Bowl win?
  a) USC
  b) Washington State
  c) UCLA
  d) Stanford

QUESTION 56: What year did OU win the national championship and not play in a bowl game?
  a) 1950
  b) 1974
  c) 1975
  d) 1985

QUESTION 57: What year was Bud Wilkinson's final year as OU head coach?
  a) 1959
  b) 1961
  c) 1963
  d) 1965

QUESTION 58: Which team did OU beat to give Bud Wilkinson his first bowl victory?
  a) North Carolina
  b) Alabama
  c) Notre Dame
  d) Tennessee

QUESTION 59: Which OU linebacker holds the school record for most tackles in one season?
- a) Brian Bosworth
- b) Rocky Calmus
- c) George Cumby
- d) Jackie Shipp

QUESTION 60: Which NFL team drafted Joe Washington in the first round of the 1976 draft?
- a) San Diego Chargers
- b) Dallas Cowboys
- c) Washington Redskins
- d) Baltimore Colts

QUESTION 61: Which year was the final year for Big Eight Conference football?
- a) 1990
- b) 1995
- c) 2000
- d) 2005

QUESTION 62: Which season was Barry Switzer's last as OU head coach?
- a) 1988
- b) 1991
- c) 1993
- d) 1995

QUESTION 63: Who was named the Most Valuable Player for the 2001 Orange Bowl where OU beat Florida State for the national championship?
- a) Josh Heupel
- b) Quentin Griffin
- c) Rocky Calmus
- d) Torrance Marshall

QUESTION 64: Which injured quarterback did Jamelle Holieway replace in 1985?
  a) Danny Bradley
  b) Troy Aikman
  c) Charles Thompson
  d) J.C. Watts

QUESTION 65: Barry Switzer's final game at OU was a loss to which team?
  a) Nebraska
  b) Texas
  c) Clemson
  d) Virginia

QUESTION 66: Which NFL Hall of Fame quarterback came to Norman in 1980 and beat OU?
  a) Joe Montana
  b) Dan Marino
  c) Jim Plunkett
  d) John Elway

QUESTION 67: In 1973, OU went 10-0-1. Which team did OU tie?
  a) USC
  b) Texas
  c) Oklahoma State
  d) Nebraska

QUESTION 68: What number did Billy Sims wear while at OU?
  a) 15
  b) 20
  c) 28
  d) 32

QUESTION 69: Which running back holds the OU record for most yards rushing in a single game?
- a) Greg Pruitt
- b) Billy Sims
- c) Steve Owens
- d) Adrian Peterson

QUESTION 70: Which Canadian Football League team did J.C. Watts play for?
- a) Edmonton
- b) Winnepeg
- c) Ottawa
- d) Montreal

QUESTION 71: Which team has twice beaten OU in the first game of a season?
- a) Alabama
- b) USC
- c) Rice
- d) TCU

QUESTION 72: Which player was a four-year starter at fullback for OU?
- a) Kenny King
- b) Lydell Carr
- c) Stanley Wilson
- d) J.D. Runnells

QUESTION 73: Which OU player holds the record for most career tackles by a lineman?
- a) Ray Hamilton
- b) Rick Bryan
- c) Tony Casilias
- d) Tommy Harris

QUESTION 74: Who was the coach of Arkansas when they beat Oklahoma in the 1978 Orange Bowl?

    a) Frank Broyles

    b) Lou Holtz

    c) Ken Hatfield

    d) Houston Nutt

QUESTION 75: Which year was Bob Stoops' first as OU head coach?

    a) 1995

    b) 1997

    c) 1999

    d) 2000

"All he did was set an NCAA freshman record with 36 touchdown tosses and lead the nation in passing efficiency. Not bad, rook, but whatcha got for an encore? How about throwing for the most touchdowns in the country, 48, with the third-most passing yards ... and a measly six interceptions ... all of which amounts to a sophomore slump like Robert Byrd is a junior senator."

— Desmond Bieler, Washington Post, writing about OU quarterback Sam Bradford's Heisman chances

QUESTION 76: Which OU player scored the only touchdown in the 2001 Orange Bowl against Florida State for the national championship?
   a) Josh Heupel
   b) Quentin Griffin
   c) Antwone Savage
   d) Torrance Marshall

QUESTION 77: What junior college did Josh Heupel play at before coming to OU?
   a) Weber State
   b) Connors State
   c) Hutchinson
   d) Snow Junior College

QUESTION 78: Keith Jackson was selected in the first round of the NFL draft by which team?
   a) Green Bay Packers
   b) Philadelphia Eagles
   c) Miami Dolphins
   d) Dallas Cowboys

QUESTION 79: Who replaced starting quarterback Rhett Bomar when he was kicked off the team before the 2006 season?
   a) Sam Bradford
   b) Paul Thompson
   c) Jason White
   d) Nate Hybl

QUESTION 80: Which OU linebacker did *NOT* win the Butkus Award?
   a) George Cumby
   b) Brain Bosworth
   c) Rocky Calmus
   d) Teddy Lehman

QUESTION 81: Which bowl game did OU play twice in the same calendar year?

    a) Cotton
    b) Orange
    c) Rose
    d) Sugar

QUESTION 82: Which is the only team to beat OU between 1985 and 1988?

    a) Texas
    b) Nebraska
    c) Miami
    d) Florida State

QUESTION 83: Which NFL team did Greg Pruitt end his career with?

    a) Cleveland Browns
    b) Los Angles Raiders
    c) Oakland Raiders
    d) Minnesota Vikings

QUESTION 84: How many games did Howard Schnellenberger win in his one season as OU head coach?

    a) Five
    b) Six
    c) Ten
    d) Eleven

QUESTION 85: What Oklahoma town is legendary Texas Longhorn head coach Darrell Royal from?

    a) Moore
    b) Ada
    c) McAlester
    d) Hollis

QUESTION 86: Which team was Bob Stoops' first loss at OU?
a) Notre Dame
b) Texas
c) Colorado
d) Nebraska

QUESTION 87: Who is the record holder for career rushing yards as a quarterback at OU?
a) Jack Mildren
b) Steve Davis
c) Thomas Lott
d) Jamelle Holieway

QUESTION 88: In 1972, Greg Pruitt finished second in the Heisman Trophy to which player?
a) Johnny Rodgers
b) Jim Plunkett
c) Pat Sullivan
d) Tony Dorsett

QUESTION 89: Jamelle Holieway's first career start came against which team?
a) Miami
b) Texas
c) Iowa State
d) Missouri

QUESTION 90: Troy Aikman's last game as a Sooner came against which team?
a) Texas
b) Miami
c) Nebraska
d) Oklahoma State

QUESTION 91: Who is the career leader at OU for interceptions?
a) Darrell Royal
b) Darrell Ray

c) Roy Williams
d) Derick Strait

QUESTION 92: Which former OU player scored on an 80-yard touchdown pass in Super Bowl XV?
a) Kenny King
b) Billy Sims
c) Greg Pruitt
d) Joe Washington

QUESTION 93: Who scored the game-winning two-point conversion that beat Florida State in the 1981 Orange Bowl?
a) Steve Rhodes
b) J.C. Watts
c) David Overstreet
d) Forest Valorea

QUESTION 94: What school did Troy Aikman transfer to after leaving OU in 1985?
a) USC
b) Washington
c) Stanford
d) UCLA

QUESTION 95: What was the length of Uwe von Schamann's winning field goal against Ohio State in 1977?
a) 35 yards
b) 41 yards
c) 47 yards
d) 50 yards

QUESTION 96: What was the school that running back Marcus Dupree transferred to when he left OU in 1983?
a) Texas
b) Mississippi
c) Mississippi State
d) Southern Mississippi

QUESTION 97: How many head coaches did OU have during the 1990s?
  a) One
  b) Two
  c) Three
  d) Four

QUESTION 98: Which team drafted OU kicker Uwe von Schamann in the 1979 NFL draft?
  a) Dallas Cowboys
  b) Chicago Bears
  c) Kansas City Chiefs
  d) Miami Dolphins

QUESTION 99: In 1979, which former OU player led the NFL in total number of receptions?
  a) Billy Brooks
  b) Joe Washington
  c) Greg Pruitt
  d) Elvis Peacock

QUESTION 100: Which OU defensive lineman holds the team record for most tackles in one season?
  a) Kevin Murphy
  b) Lee Roy Selmon
  c) Reggie Kinlaw
  d) Rick Bryan

QUESTION 101: Who led the Sooners in rushing yards in 1987?
  a) Jamelle Holieway
  b) Lydell Carr
  c) Patrick Collins
  d) Anthony Stafford

QUESTION 102: Who led the Sooners in all-purpose yards for 1976?
 a) Thomas Lott
 b) Billy Sims
 c) Kenny King
 d) Horace Ivory

"Football doesn't build character—it
eliminates weak ones."
— Darrell Royal

QUESTION 103: Which former OU receiver went to the NFL Pro Bowl in 2000?
 a) Keith Jackson
 b) Cory Warren
 c) Mark Clayton
 d) Stephen Alexander

QUESTION 104: Which was the only team to beat OU in 1972?
 a) Colorado
 b) USC
 c) Texas
 d) Nebraska

QUESTION 105: Which team drafted Steve Owens in the 1970 NFL draft?
 a) Dallas Cowboys
 b) Minnesota Vikings
 c) Detroit Lions
 d) Denver Broncos

QUESTION 106: Which OU quarterback did not wear No. 1 on his jersey?
   a) Danny Bradley
   b) Steve Davis
   c) J.C. Watts
   d) Eric Moore

QUESTION 107: Which was the first team that Barry Switzer lost to as head coach?
   a) USC
   b) Kansas
   c) Texas
   d) Nebraska

QUESTION 108: Who is the only player to rush for more than 200 yards in three games as a freshman?
   a) Billy Sims
   b) Marcus Dupree
   c) Mike Gaddis
   d) Adrian Peterson

QUESTION 109: Which OU receiver eclipsed 1,000 receiving yards faster than any other Sooner?
   a) Keith Jackson
   b) Mark Clayton
   c) Malcolm Kelly
   d) Ryan Broyles

QUESTION 110: In 2004, Adrian Peterson finished second in the Heisman Trophy voting to which player?
   a) Jason White
   b) Matt Leinart
   c) Reggie Bush
   d) Larry Fitzgerald

QUESTION 111: When Billy Sims won the Heisman Trophy in 1978 he led the country in rushing yards and which other category?
a) Total offense
b) Scoring
c) Receiving yards
d) Kick return yards

QUESTION 112: Which player scored the final touchdown in OU's national championship victory over Penn State in the 1986 Orange Bowl?
a) Spencer Tillman
b) Jamelle Holieway
c) Keith Jackson
d) Lydell Carr

QUESTION 113: Who was Barry Switzer's first starting quarterback as head coach?
a) Jack Mildren
b) Steve Davis
c) Thomas Lott
d) J.C. Watts

QUESTION 114: Which player scored six touchdowns in one game?
a) Billy Sims
b) Joe Washington
c) Quentin Griffin
d) Adrian Peterson

QUESTION 115: What year did OU win its first Big 12 conference title?
a) 1996
b) 1999
c) 2000
d) 2003

QUESTION 116: Which U.S. President appointed Bud Wilkinson as head of the national task force on health?
   a) Eisenhower
   b) Kennedy
   c) Nixon
   d) Reagan

QUESTION 117: At which school did Barry Switzer play college ball?
   a) Oklahoma
   b) Arkansas
   c) Texas
   d) Kansas

QUESTION 118: Which Heisman Trophy winner did not play high school football in Oklahoma?
   a) Billy Sims
   b) Steve Owens
   c) Jason White
   d) Billy Vessels

QUESTION 119: The 1978 starting backfield at OU did *NOT* consist of which player?
   a) Thomas Lott
   b) Kenny King
   c) David Overstreet
   d) Horace Ivory

QUESTION 120: At which school did Bob Stoops play college ball?
   a) Oklahoma
   b) Maryland
   c) North Carolina
   d) Iowa

QUESTION 121: The Selmon brothers come from which Oklahoma town?
   a) Tulsa
   b) Eufaula
   c) Elk City
   d) Ada

QUESTION 122: Head coach John Blake was at what position during his OU playing days?
   a) Running back
   b) Nose guard
   c) Linebacker
   d) Center

QUESTION 123: Howard Schnellenberger was at what school before coming to OU in 1995?
   a) Miami
   b) Louisville
   c) Kentucky
   d) Alabama

QUESTION 124: Before taking over as head coach, Barry Switzer coached what position at OU?
   a) Offensive coordinator
   b) Defensive coordinator
   c) Linebackers
   d) Special teams

QUESTION 125: Bob Stoops came from which school to OU?
   a) Georgia
   b) Alabama
   c) Florida State
   d) Florida

QUESTION 126: OU has beaten which team three times in the Orange Bowl?
   a) Florida State
   b) Penn State
   c) Michigan
   d) USC

"They brought me in to win games—not to run a (expletive) church camp."
— Bob Stoops

QUESTION 127: In OU's only Rose Bowl appearance, the Sooners defeated which team?
   a) Michigan
   b) Washington State
   c) Ohio State
   d) UCLA

QUESTION 128: Brian Bosworth went to high school in which Texas city?
   a) Fort Worth
   b) Houston
   c) Iving
   d) Austin

QUESTION 129: Who was the OU head coach before Barry Switzer?
   a) Bud Wilkinson
   b) Gomer Jones
   c) Jim McKenzie
   d) Chuck Fairbanks

QUESTION 130: Chuck Fairbanks left OU to be the head coach of which NFL team?
  a) New England Patriots
  b) Dallas Cowboys
  c) Pittsburgh Steelers
  d) New Orleans Saints

QUESTION 131: Which former OU quarterback was the number one pick of the draft by the Dallas Cowboys?
  a) Sam Bradford
  b) Jason White
  c) Troy Aikman
  d) Josh Heupel

QUESTION 132: What year did all three Selmon brothers start on the defensive line together?
  a) 1971
  b) 1973
  c) 1975
  d) 1978

QUESTION 133: Who replaced an injured Jamelle Holieway at quarterback in 1987?
  a) Troy Aikman
  b) Charles Thompson
  c) Eric Mitchell
  d) David Vickers

QUESTION 134: What state did Jamelle Holieway play high school football in?
  a) Oklahoma
  b) Texas
  c) Florida
  d) California

QUESTION 135: What team beat OU in the 1985 Orange Bowl?
   a) Miami
   b) Penn State
   c) USC
   d) Washington

QUESTION 136: Who was OU's first Heisman Trophy winner?
   a) Billy Vessels
   b) Steve Owens
   c) Billy Sims
   d) Jason White

QUESTION 137: What Oklahoma high school did Jason White play for?
   a) Norman
   b) Tuttle
   c) Eufaula
   d) Ardmore

QUESTION 138: Which team did OU beat twice during the 2000 national championship season?
   a) Texas
   b) Nebraska
   c) Missouri
   d) Kansas State

QUESTION 139: Who was the OU quarterback in the 1975 national championship season?
   a) Jack Mildren
   b) Steve Davis
   c) Thomas Lott
   d) J.C. Watts

QUESTION 140: What team did OU play the day after President Kennedy's assassination in 1963?
   a) Texas
   b) Colorado

c) Oklahoma State
d) Nebraska

QUESTION 141: Which OU coach went on to coach the Dallas Cowboys to a Super Bowl victory?
a) Bud Wilkinson
b) Chuck Fairbanks
c) Barry Switzer
d) Gary Gibbs

QUESTION 142: Which former OU player hired John Blake as head coach?
a) Gary Gibbs
b) Steve Owens
c) Darrell Royal
d) Steve Davis

QUESTION 143: On what holiday did OU and Nebraska usually play on?
a) Labor Day
b) Halloween
c) Thanksgiving
d) Christmas

QUESTION 144: Who is the only OU quarterback to win a Super Bowl?
a) Jack Mildren
b) Thomas Lott
c) Troy Aikman
d) Josh Heupel

QUESTION 145: Which former OU kicker made fields goals in a Super Bowl?
a) Uwe von Schamann
b) Scott Blanton
c) Tim Lashar
d) Garrick Hartley

QUESTION 146: Which player returned a kickoff 89 yards for a touchdown against Notre Dame in 1999?
- a) J. T. Thatcher
- b) Brandon Daniels
- c) Quentin Griffin
- d) Antwone Savage

QUESTION 147: What year did OU play for the national championship in both football and basketball?
- a) 1950
- b) 1977
- c) 1988
- d) 2003

QUESTION 148: What was OU's first bowl game?
- a) Orange
- b) Sugar
- c) Cotton
- d) Rose

QUESTION 149: Who did OU play in its first bowl game?
- a) Michigan
- b) North Carolina
- c) Georgia
- d) Tennessee

QUESTION 150: Who wrote *Bootleggers Boy*?
- a) Bud Wilkinson
- b) Barry Switzer
- c) Charles Thompson
- d) Brian Bosworth

QUESTION 151: Who leads OU in career rushing yards?
- a) Adrian Peterson
- b) Joe Washington
- c) Steve Owens
- d) Billy Sims

"The history of Oklahoma is about winning championships. We already have six national championships, now we have seven ... you can't say, 'well that was then, this is now.' That's Oklahoma football"
— Bob Stoops

QUESTION 152: Who is OU's single season rushing leader?
- a) Adrian Peterson
- b) Joe Washington
- c) Steve Owens
- d) Billy Sims

QUESTION 153: Who is the record holder for most rushing yards in a game?
- a) Adrian Peterson
- b) Billy Sims
- c) Greg Pruitt
- d) Demond Parker

QUESTION 154: Who is OU's career passing leader?
- a) Jason White
- b) Sam Bradford
- c) Josh Heupel
- d) Landry Jones

QUESTION 155: Who holds the OU record for most yards passing in a season?
   a) Landry Jones
   b) Sam Bradford
   c) Jason White
   d) Nate Hybl

QUESTION 156: Which receiver holds the record for most yards in a career?
   a) Mark Clayton
   b) Malcoln Kelly
   c) Keith Jackson
   d) Ryan Broyles

QUESTION 157: Who holds the record for most receiving yards in a season?
   a) Mark Clayton
   b) Malcolm Kelly
   c) Jermaine Gresham
   d) Ryan Broyles

QUESTION 158: Who holds the record for most receiving yards in one game?
   a) Mark Clayton
   b) Brandon Jones
   c) P.J. Mills
   d) Ryan Broyles

QUESTION 159: Who is the all-time scoring leader in OU history?
   a) Billy Sims
   b) J.C. Watts
   c) Uwe von Schamann
   d) DeMarco Murray

QUESTION 160: Who is the career leader in extra points made?
a) Uwe von Schamann
b) Scott Blanton
c) R. D. Lashar
d) Tim Lashar

QUESTION 161: Who is the quarterback with the most career wins?
a) Jason White
b) Steve Davis
c) Thomas Lott
d) Jamelle Holieway

QUESTION 162: Which team scored the most points against OU in a game?
a) Texas
b) USC
c) Nebraska
d) Kansas State

QUESTION 163: Which school does OU have the most wins against?
a) Oklahoma State
b) Kansas
c) Kansas State
d) Texas

QUESTION 164: Which school was not a member of the Big 8 Conference?
a) Texas
b) Oklahoma State
c) Kansas
d) Missouri

QUESTION 165: Which state has OU never had a player from?
   a) Utah
   b) West Virginia
   c) Wyoming
   d) Hawaii

QUESTION 166: OU recruits most of its players from Oklahoma and Texas. Outside of those two states, which state has sent the most players to OU?
   a) California
   b) Florida
   c) Arkansas
   d) Missouri

QUESTION 167: What year was artificial turf placed in OU's stadium?
   a) 1950
   b) 1960
   c) 1970
   d) 1980

QUESTION 168: What year was artificial turf removed?
   a) 1975
   b) 1986
   c) 1994
   d) 2000

QUESTION 169: Which head coach was the fastest to reach 100 wins?
   a) Bennie Owen
   b) Bud Wilkinson
   c) Barry Switzer
   d) Bob Stoops

QUESTION 170: Which school has OU faced the most in bowl games?
- a) Penn State
- b) Washington
- c) Florida State
- d) Arkansas

QUESTION 171: Which OU kicker kicked bare-footed?
- a) Uwe von Schamann
- b) Michael Keeling
- c) R.D. Lashar
- d) Scott Blanton

QUESTION 172: What number did Steve Owens wear?
- a) 22
- b) 32
- c) 36
- d) 44

QUESTION 173: Who did Sam Bradford beat out for the 2008 Heisman Trophy?
- a) Tim Tebow
- b) Colt McCoy
- c) Michael Crabtree
- d) Shonn Greene

QUESTION 174: In 1986, Brian Bosworth finished fourth in the Heisman Trophy voting. Who won the Heisman that year?
- a) Jim Harbaugh
- b) D.J. Dozier
- c) Paul Palmer
- d) Vinny Testaverde

QUESTION 175: In 2000, Josh Heupel came in second in the Heisman voting ... but beat the Heisman winner when it mattered most. Which quarterback won the Heisman over Heupel but then lost to him in the Orange Bowl?
  a) Drew Brees
  b) Chris Weinke
  c) Michael Vick
  d) Marques Tuiasosopo

QUESTION 176: Which head coach won his first four games?
  a) Bob Stoops
  b) Barry Switzer
  c) Jim Mackenzie
  d) Bennie Owen

"At Oklahoma, we never punted."
— Jerry Tubbs, All-American center, after he snapped the ball over a punter's head during an All-Star game

---

QUESTION 177: Billy Sims best rushing game was 282 yards. Who was it against?
  a) Texas
  b) Oklahoma State
  c) Missouri
  d) Nebraska

QUESTION 178: Greg Pruitt has the single-game rushing record of 294 yards. Who was it against?
  a) Texas
  b) Kansas State

c) Iowa State
d) Nebraska

QUESTION 179: What was Jack Mildren's jersey number?
  a) 1
  b) 7
  c) 11
  d) 14

QUESTION 180: Who was Barry Switzer's first starting quarterback?
  a) Thomas Lott
  b) Steve Davis
  c) Jack Mildren
  d) J.C. Watts

QUESTION 181: Which team snapped OU's 47-game winning streak in 1957?
  a) Notre Dame
  b) Texas
  c) Alabama
  d) Nebraska

QUESTION 182: What high school did Sam Bradford attend?
  a) Ardmore
  b) Muskogee
  c) Pauls Valley
  d) Putnam City North

QUESTION 183: Before coming to OU, Barry Switzer coached at which university?
  a) Alabama
  b) Arkansas
  c) Kansas
  d) Texas

QUESTION 184: What elected office was Jack Mildren voted into in 1990?
   a) Governor
   b) Senator
   c) Attorney general
   d) Lieutenant governor

QUESTION 185: Who was a four-year starter at tight end?
   a) Victor Hicks
   b) Keith Jackson
   c) Stephen Alexander
   d) Trent Smith

QUESTION 186: Which linebacker started alongside Brian Bosworth for three years?
   a) Rocky Calmus
   b) George Cumby
   c) Paul Migliazzo
   d) Donte Jones

QUESTION 187: Which defensive back had three interceptions in the 1980 Orange Bowl?
   a) Darrell Ray
   b) Bud Hebert
   c) Jay Jimerson
   d) Basil Banks

QUESTION 188: Who kicked the game-winning field goal with just seconds left against Oklahoma State in 1983?
   a) Uwe von Schamann
   b) Tim Lashar
   c) R.D. Lashar
   d) Scott Blanton

QUESTION 189: Who leads OU in career all-purpose yards?
   a) Joe Washington
   b) Billy Sims

   c) Quentin Griffin
   d) DeMarco Murray

QUESTION 190: What year did OU have the most wins?
   a) 1955
   b) 1974
   c) 1985
   d) 2000

QUESTION 191: How many Big 12 Conference championships has OU won?
   a) 5
   b) 7
   c) 9
   d) 11

"They're scared, men ... scared men on a scared team."
— Barry Switzer, pre-game speech, OU vs. Texas

QUESTION 192: Barry Switzer was offensive coordinator for which OU head coach?
   a) Bud Wilkinson
   b) Gomer Jones
   c) Jim Mackenzie
   d) Chuck Fairbanks

QUESTION 193: OU's football stadium is on which side of campus?
- a) North
- b) South
- c) East
- d) West

QUESTION 194: What street is the stadium on?
- a) Boyd
- b) Elm
- c) College
- d) Jenkins

OKLAHOMA 195: The Barry Switzer Center opened in what year?
- a) 1973
- b) 1985
- c) 1999
- d) 2005

QUESTION 196: Bob Stoops won his first national championship in what year of coaching OU?
- a) First
- b) Second
- c) Third
- d) Fourth

QUESTION 197: Which defensive back was a first round draft choice by the Dallas Cowboys in 2002?
- a) Darrell Ray
- b) Ricky Dixon
- c) Roy Williams
- d) Brodney Pool

QUESTION 198: John Blake hired which current NFL coach to be his defensive coordinator?
- a) Pete Carroll
- b) Andy Reid
- c) Lovie Smith
- d) Rex Ryan

QUESTION 199: How many seasons was John Blake head coach at OU?
- a) One
- b) Three
- c) Five
- d) Seven

QUESTION 200: What was Bob Stoops' first bowl game at OU?
- a) Independence
- b) Orange
- c) Fiesta
- d) Sugar

Oklahoma Sooners Trivia IQ
Answer Key

___ QUESTION 1: D
___ QUESTION 2: B
___ QUESTION 3: D
___ QUESTION 4: A
___ QUESTION 5: C
___ QUESTION 6: B
___ QUESTION 7: D
___ QUESTION 8: A
___ QUESTION 9: B
___ QUESTION 10: D
___ QUESTION 11: A
___ QUESTION 12: A
___ QUESTION 13: C
___ QUESTION 14: B
___ QUESTION 15: C
___ QUESTION 16: D
___ QUESTION 17: A
___ QUESTION 18: D
___ QUESTION 19: C
___ QUESTION 20: B
___ QUESTION 21: C
___ QUESTION 22: B
___ QUESTION 23: D
___ QUESTION 24: A
___ QUESTION 25: C
___ QUESTION 26: B
___ QUESTION 27: A
___ QUESTION 28: A
___ QUESTION 29: B
___ QUESTION 30: D
___ QUESTION 31: C
___ QUESTION 32: C
___ QUESTION 33: A

___ **QUESTION 34:** A
___ **QUESTION 35:** C
___ **QUESTION 36:** A
___ **QUESTION 37:** D
___ **QUESTION 38:** C
___ **QUESTION 39:** A
___ **QUESTION 40:** D
___ **QUESTION 41:** B
___ **QUESTION 42:** C
___ **QUESTION 43:** D
___ **QUESTION 44:** A
___ **QUESTION 45:** A
___ **QUESTION 46:** D
___ **QUESTION 47:** A
___ **QUESTION 48:** B
___ **QUESTION 49:** B
___ **QUESTION 50:** C
___ **QUESTION 51:** D
___ **QUESTION 52:** A
___ **QUESTION 53:** B
___ **QUESTION 54:** D
___ **QUESTION 55:** B
___ **QUESTION 56:** B
___ **QUESTION 57:** C
___ **QUESTION 58:** A
___ **QUESTION 59:** D
___ **QUESTION 60:** A
___ **QUESTION 61:** B
___ **QUESTION 62:** A
___ **QUESTION 63:** D
___ **QUESTION 64:** B
___ **QUESTION 65:** C
___ **QUESTION 66:** D
___ **QUESTION 67:** A
___ **QUESTION 68:** B
___ **QUESTION 69:** A
___ **QUESTION 70:** C

___ **QUESTION 71:** D
___ **QUESTION 72:** B
___ **QUESTION 73:** B
___ **QUESTION 74:** B
___ **QUESTION 75:** C
___ **QUESTION 76:** B
___ **QUESTION 77:** D
___ **QUESTION 78:** B
___ **QUESTION 79:** B
___ **QUESTION 80:** A
___ **QUESTION 81:** D
___ **QUESTION 82:** C
___ **QUESTION 83:** B
___ **QUESTION 84:** A
___ **QUESTION 85:** D
___ **QUESTION 86:** A
___ **QUESTION 87:** D
___ **QUESTION 88:** A
___ **QUESTION 89:** C
___ **QUESTION 90:** B
___ **QUESTION 91:** A
___ **QUESTION 92:** A
___ **QUESTION 93:** D
___ **QUESTION 94:** D
___ **QUESTION 95:** B
___ **QUESTION 96:** D
___ **QUESTION 97:** D
___ **QUESTION 98:** D
___ **QUESTION 99:** B
___ **QUESTION 100:** A
___ **QUESTION 101:** A
___ **QUESTION 102:** C
___ **QUESTION 103:** D
___ **QUESTION 104:** A
___ **QUESTION 105:** C
___ **QUESTION 106:** B
___ **QUESTION 107:** B

___ **QUESTION 108:** D
___ **QUESTION 109:** C
___ **QUESTION 110:** B
___ **QUESTION 111:** B
___ **QUESTION 112:** D
___ **QUESTION 113:** B
___ **QUESTION 114:** C
___ **QUESTION 115:** C
___ **QUESTION 116:** B
___ **QUESTION 117:** B
___ **QUESTION 118:** A
___ **QUESTION 119:** D
___ **QUESTION 120:** D
___ **QUESTION 121:** B
___ **QUESTION 122:** B
___ **QUESTION 123:** B
___ **QUESTION 124:** A
___ **QUESTION 125:** D
___ **QUESTION 126:** A
___ **QUESTION 127:** B
___ **QUESTION 128:** C
___ **QUESTION 129:** D
___ **QUESTION 130:** A
___ **QUESTION 131:** C
___ **QUESTION 132:** B
___ **QUESTION 133:** B
___ **QUESTION 134:** D
___ **QUESTION 135:** D
___ **QUESTION 136:** A
___ **QUESTION 137:** B
___ **QUESTION 138:** D
___ **QUESTION 139:** B
___ **QUESTION 140:** D
___ **QUESTION 141:** C
___ **QUESTION 142:** B
___ **QUESTION 143:** C
___ **QUESTION 144:** C

___ **QUESTION 145:** D
___ **QUESTION 146:** B
___ **QUESTION 147:** C
___ **QUESTION 148:** A
___ **QUESTION 149:** D
___ **QUESTION 150:** B
___ **QUESTION 151:** D
___ **QUESTION 152:** A
___ **QUESTION 153:** C
___ **QUESTION 154:** B
___ **QUESTION 155:** B
___ **QUESTION 156:** D
___ **QUESTION 157:** D
___ **QUESTION 158:** D
___ **QUESTION 159:** D
___ **QUESTION 160:** C
___ **QUESTION 161:** B
___ **QUESTION 162:** C
___ **QUESTION 163:** A
___ **QUESTION 164:** A
___ **QUESTION 165:** B
___ **QUESTION 166:** A
___ **QUESTION 167:** C
___ **QUESTION 168:** C
___ **QUESTION 169:** B
___ **QUESTION 170:** C
___ **QUESTION 171:** B
___ **QUESTION 172:** C
___ **QUESTION 173:** B
___ **QUESTION 174:** D
___ **QUESTION 175:** B
___ **QUESTION 176:** C
___ **QUESTION 177:** C
___ **QUESTION 178:** B
___ **QUESTION 179:** C
___ **QUESTION 180:** B
___ **QUESTION 181:** A

___ **QUESTION 182:** D
___ **QUESTION 183:** B
___ **QUESTION 184:** D
___ **QUESTION 185:** B
___ **QUESTION 186:** C
___ **QUESTION 187:** B
___ **QUESTION 188:** B
___ **QUESTION 189:** D
___ **QUESTION 190:** D
___ **QUESTION 191:** B
___ **QUESTION 192:** D
___ **QUESTION 193:** C
___ **QUESTION 194:** D
___ **QUESTION 195:** C
___ **QUESTION 196:** B
___ **QUESTION 197:** C
___ **QUESTION 198:** D
___ **QUESTION 199:** B
___ **QUESTION 200:** A

Got your total? Here's how your score breaks down:

A BOOMER SOONER	= 190 – 200
A FANATIC	= 180 – 189
A FAN	= 170 – 179
A FAIR WEATHER FAN	= 160 – 169
A GAME DAY FAN	= 150 – 159
A TEXAS LONGHORN	= 149 OR LESS

Think you can do better? Be on the lookout for *Oklahoma Sooners Trivia IQ, Volume II.*

About the Authors

SCOTT COOPER is an award-winning journalist who has lived in Norman, Oklahoma for 27 years. He is a graduate of the University of Oklahoma.

KEITH GADDIE lives in Norman, Oklahoma, where he writes and teaches at the University of Oklahoma. Among his published books are *The University of Georgia Football* (Savas-Beatie), *Georgia Bulldogs IQ* (Black Mesa, with Kim Gaddie), *Born to Run*, and the novel *Ghosts on Vintners Landing* (Black Mesa).

References

- soonersports.com
- oklahoma.rivals.com
- ouinsider.com
- espn.com
- foxsports.com
- Yahoo Sports!
- cbssports.com
- newsok.com
- tulsaworld.com
- soonerstats.com

About Black Mesa

BLACK MESA IS a Florida-based publishing company that specializes in sports history and trivia books. Look for these popular titles in our trivia IQ series:

- *Mixed Martial Arts (Volumes I & II)*
- *Boston Red Sox (Volumes I & II)*
- *Tampa Bay Rays*
- *New York Yankees*
- *Atlanta Braves*
- *Major League Baseball*
- *Milwaukee Brewers*
- *St. Louis Cardinals*
- *Cincinnati Reds*
- *Boston Celtics*
- *Florida Gators Football*
- *Georgia Bulldogs Football (Keith Gaddie)*
- *Texas Longhorns Football*
- *Texas A&M Aggies Football*
- *New England Patriots*

For information about special discounts for bulk purchases, please email:

black.mesa.publishing@gmail.com

www.blackmesabooks.com

Sports by the Numbers Series

- *Major League Baseball*
- *New York Yankees*
- *Boston Red Sox*
- *San Francisco Giants*
- *Texas Rangers*
- *University of Oklahoma Football*
- *University of Georgia Football (Keith Gaddie)*
- *Penn State University Football*
- *NASCAR*
- *Sacramento Kings Basketball*
- *Mixed Martial Arts*

Available Soon

- *Los Angeles Dodgers*
- *Boston Celtics*
- *Dallas Cowboys*

Made in the USA
Lexington, KY
04 December 2016